ghostly frights for halloween nights

ghostly frights for halloween nights

Shauna Mooney Kawasaki

Sterling Publishing Co., Inc. New York
A Sterling / Chapelle Book

Chapelle, Ltd.:
   • Owner: Jo Packham
   • Editor: Laura Best
   • Illustrator: Shauna Mooney Kawasaki
   • Photographer: Kevin Dilley, Hazen Photography

   • Staff: Areta Bingham, Kass Burchett, Marilyn Goff, Holly Hollingsworth,
      Susan Jorgensen, Barbara Milburn, Linda Orton, Karmen Quinney,
      Cindy Stoeckl, Kim Taylor, Sara Toliver, Kristi Torsak

Library of Congress Cataloging-in-Publication Data

Kawasaki, Shauna Mooney.
   Ghostly frights for Halloween nights / Shauna Mooney Kawasaki.
      p. cm.
   "A Sterling/Chapelle book."
   ISBN 0-8069-5829-4 Hardcover
   ISBN 1-4027-0118-7 Paperback
      1. Halloween decorations. 2. Handicraft. I. Title.

   TT900.H32 K39 2001
   745.594'1646--dc21   2001032016

                10 9 8 7 6 5 4 3 2 1

First paperback edition published in 2002 by
Sterling Publishing Company, Inc.
387 Park Avenue South, New York, NY 10016
©2001 by Shauna Mooney Kawasaki
Distributed in Canada by Sterling Publishing
C/o Canadian Manda Group, One Atlantic Avenue, Suite 105
Toronto, Ontario, Canada M6K 3E7
Distributed in Australia by Capricorn Link (Australia) Pty Ltd.
P.O. Box 704, Windsor, NSW 2756 Australia
Printed in China
All Rights Reserved

         Sterling ISBN 0-8069-5829-4 Hardcover
         Sterling ISBN 1-4027-0118-7 Paperback

If you have any questions or comments, please contact:
Chapelle, Ltd., Inc., P.O. Box 9252, Ogden, UT 84409
         (801) 621-2777 • (801) 621-2788 Fax
chapelle@chapelleltd.com • www.chapelleltd.com

About the Author

Shauna Mooney Kawasaki was born October 20, 1953, in Provo, Utah, with a pencil in one hand, a pen in the other, and a paintbrush behind her ear. Though she made it through high school, with the encouragement of her mother, she taught herself to draw, write, sew, carve, garden, and make her own toys. These passions "possess" her to this day.

Her professional career began in advertising, but was short-lived when her artistic talents were discovered by others. She was asked to be the art director for a national children's magazine and she enjoyed this position for 18 years.

She lived as a happy and content old-maid-auntie until age 37, when she married Michael Kawasaki and his seven wonderful children. This union did not slow Shauna down. Since her move to work-at-home mom, she has been involved in writing, illustrating, and designing over 20 books. Her passions have broadened into painting murals for hands-on exhibits in children's museums, traveling, gardening, reading, and watching movies—especially scary ones. She relaxes from her busy schedule by sewing dolls for herself, her family, and for profit.

Shauna loves monsters, robots, little children, vintage sports cars, antique jewelry, eating, and teasing anyone—whether she knows them or not.

Dedicated to the mummy, Dracula, Frankenstein's monster, and Norman (1927–2000)—all of whom believe in life after death.

INTRODUCTION

What makes Halloween such a great holiday? Is it the cozy feeling as days get shorter and nights get longer? Or the warmth we feel, smelling pumpkin cookies? Maybe it's the excitement little children share while deciding what to dress up as on Halloween. Or is it a celebration of the end of summer and the beginning of winter? Perhaps it's simply that we enjoy being scared, and scaring! This book is to help you scare someone, and be a little scared yourself. But, the main *ghouls* of this book are . . .

- To provide fast and easy projects you can make alone or with children.

- To provide project ideas that are easy to put up, take down, and store until next year.

- To provide projects that are not cute, but daringly different and a little bit frightening.

- To describe projects made with materials found around your house, or that can be purchased at a craft store, discount store, second-hand store, or remnant bin.

Warning: Don't feel panic, uneasiness, or horror
when you begin one of these petrifying projects—simply have frightful fun.

TABLE OF CONTENTS

We enjoy making our homes *comfortable* and **inviting** for family and friends.

But once a year we **rebel and** mischievously turn our **innocent** homes into terrifying, creepy places. Our imaginations run *wild,* while offering goodies and **tricks** to those who dare **haunt** our doorstep.

eerie entry

spirit tissues

Enlarge Large Ghost and Small Ghost (page 11) patterns as needed. Cut out several ghosts from tissue paper, making different shapes, positions, and sizes. Take one ghost at a time and wad up paper as tightly as possible. Smooth out paper and tape to mirrors and windows.

SMALL GHOST

wary window

With things found around your house, decorate your most prominent window. Using thumbtacks, tack old, dusty lace around the window frame. Drape tattered strips of fabric around window corners. Tangle together string and yarn and loop it around the window. Tack Christmas lights around the window and cover with pieces of batting. Hang Dem–dough-bones (page 93) in corners or use them for the tiebacks. Arrange Spirit Tissues (page 10) so as to peek out from corners or come up from windowsills. String artificial spiderwebs around window corners.

grim reaper

Cover head with wet, torn white paper. Let dry.

Cut out spooky eyes, inverted "V" for nose, and grimacing mouth from black paper. Cut a small hole in top of head.

Cut 2" from toilet tissue roll and slide over hook of hanger. Tie a loop of fishing line to hanger and thread it up through head and through hole in top. Drape black fabric over head and pin in place around face. Drape black fabric over hanger. Pad if necessary, then pin in place. Pin rubber gloves in sleeves or opening in front.

Cut a scythe blade from cardboard. Tape blade to end of walking stick and attach to reaper's hands. Hang reaper outside where the wind can catch him. He looks like he is floating around ready to snatch you at any moment.

Your front door is the entry to Scaryland. If your door is white or wood, cover it with black crepe paper—unless you can see a terrifying way to make it come alive. If your door is already dark—all the better, because it looks like a big hole anyway. Design a face for your door, using the examples to the left.

daunting door

WHAT DO WITCHES PUT ON THEIR FRONT DOORS?

WARLOCKS.

Lightly draw drops of blood and a mouth on red card stock. Draw monster teeth and eerie eyeballs on white card stock. Be certain they are big—small features look wimpy. Tape features to the door and hope it doesn't scare the mail carrier away!

TRICK OR TREAT PRANKS

SURPRISE YOUR HALLOWEEN GUESTS BY DRESSING UP SCARIER THAN THEM— WHITE MAKE-UP, DARK EYES, PHONY TEETH, WIGS, RUBBER GLOVES, WITCH HATS & FALSE NOSES.

LIE FLAT ON THE GROUND OR HIDE BEHIND SOME BUSHES, AND AT THE RIGHT TIME, ARISE AND LIFT UP THE GRIM REAPER THAT YOU HAVE ATTACHED TO A POLE. REAL CREEPY!

HAIR DRYER.

COOL

HEAVY PLASTIC BAG

FABRIC SLEEVE

COTTON GLOVE

- DRY ICE IN A BUCKET OF WARM WATER WILL MAKE FOG BY YOUR FRONT DOOR.
- PLASTIC GROCERY BAGS, TIED WITH A THREAD, WILL BLOW WILDLY IN THE WIND.
- COVER A HELIUM-FILLED BALLOON IN LIGHTWEIGHT WHITE CLOTH, ATTACH BLACK CUT-OUT FACIAL FEATURES WITH TAPE AND FLOAT YOUR GHOST AROUND THE YARD.

GET OUT THE OLD FISHING POLE & PUT YOUR FAVORITE CHAIR IN FRONT OF A SECOND STORY WINDOW FACING THE FRONT OF THE HOUSE. ON THE END OF THE LINE PUT A PLASTIC BAT, SPIDER, GAUZE GHOST, OR ATTACH IT TO A LOW BRANCH OR BUSH AND MAKE IT JUMP & JIGGLE AT THE TRICK-OR-TREATERS.

- MAKE A SCARY WAVING ARM BY FOLLOWING DIAGRAM ABOVE. PRETEND TO HAND OUT THOSE LITTLE TREATS— AND THEY WILL DROP WHEN THE POWER GOES OFF.

- PAINT BLOODY RED (TEMPERA) FOOTPRINTS LEADING UP TO THE PORCH.
- USE BLACK LIGHTS & WHITE SHEETS WHERE TRICK-OR-TREATERS CAN SEE THEM.
- USE SCARY TAPES OR CD'S FOR BACKGROUND SOUNDS—OOOOEEEOOOOO!

Materials
Berries on a limb
Craft knife
½" Dowel
Large terra-cotta pot
Old bones
Pine boughs
Pumpkins: large (1),
   medium (1), small (1)
Ribbons
Rocks or dirt
Scary sticks

Break stems off large and medium pumpkins. Cut hole through top and bottom of large and medium pumpkins.

Push dowel through cut holes and place pumpkins in terra-cotta pot. Arrange rocks or dirt around dowel in bottom of pot to steady pumpkins.

Cut hole in bottom of small pumpkin and place on top of dowel, so as to rest on top of second pumpkin. Shorten dowel as needed.

Embellish arrangement with berries on the limb, old bones, pine boughs, ribbons, and scary sticks.

skull banner

Materials

Clothesline, 12'
Fabrics: black, 20" x 60"
   muslin, 16" x 20"
   white, 1 yd
Fusible bonding, 1 yd

Iron & ironing board
Needle & black thread
Pencil
Pins
Scissors

The myth of the skeleton dates back to when tribal people preserved the heads or skulls of their ancestors, which they painted, dressed, and displayed in their homes. After time, organized religion frowned on this practice. Today, the Day of the Dead, a Mexican celebration, is celebrated on the eve of October 3. This holiday is a happy one, filled with color, parades, costumes, and feasting. Alters are set up in homes to honor members of the family who have passed away. The alter is the power point, acting as a door between the living and the dead.

SKULL

1. Tear black fabric into 20" x 10" flags. Tear muslin into 20" x 1" strips. Fray edges of flags and strips.

2. Apply fusible bonding to white fabric, following manufacturer's instructions. Fold and pin fabric into sixths.

3. Using Skull pattern, lightly draw skull (minus the mouth) onto bonding. Cut out all six at one time. Refer to face ideas on page 18. One at a time, cut out "angry" eye holes and an inverted "V" for nose.

4. Make a cut for mouth and jaw. Position jaw 1" above bottom of flag. Place skull ½" above jaw. Bond in place and repeat for remaining flags.

5. Fold top of flag over 5" onto face side of flag. Stitch across flag ¾" down from fold. Tie two muslin strips in the center of the clothesline. Thread the line through the flags, three on each side. Tie two more strips between each flag and three on each end. Hang line in front of your home to honor family members who have passed away.

werewolf masks

Materials
Craft glue
½" Elastic banding, 4'
Felt squares: brown, tan (2 each)
Fur fabrics: brown, tan (¼ yd each)
Needle & crochet thread
Pins
Ribbon
Sharp-tipped scissors

Using Mask patterns on page 21, pin patterns on wrong side of fur. Cut two brown and two tan masks. Make small, short cuts to leave as much fur intact as possible. Pin mask patterns onto felt squares. Cut four masks from felt. Glue felt in place on back side of masks. Refer to How to Stitch on page 93. Blanket–stitch around entire mask, including eyeholes and nose pieces. Fold masks in half, fur side out, and stitch along fold to make permanent crease. Sew nose pieces onto masks. Alternate noses so each mask looks different.

Cut 24" pieces of ribbon and sew several at a time to each side. Cut one 12" piece from elastic for each mask. Sew one end to each side of each mask. Push fur out of eye holes before wearing.

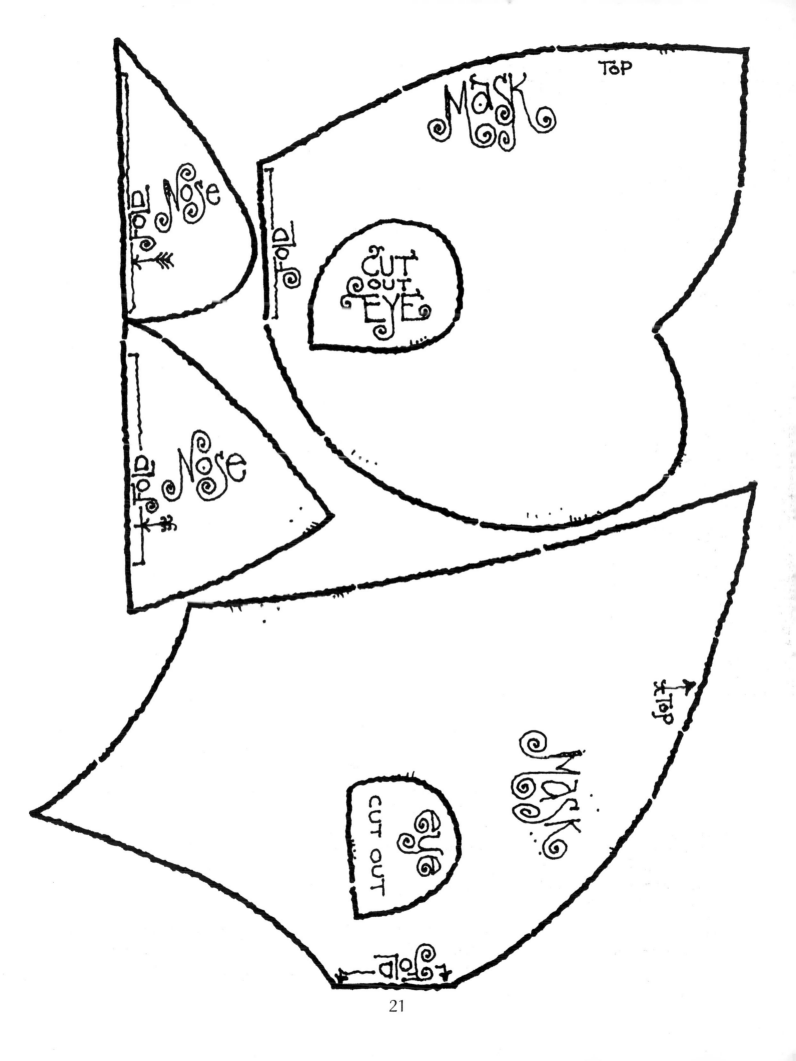

anxietree

Paint large terra-cotta pot black. Let dry. Turn pot over and center cheesecloth over pot. Sponge decoupage medium over cloth and position it on the sides of the pot like mist coming up from the swamps. Tuck leaves in, on, and around the cloth like they are floating. Let dry. Position a branch in pot and surround with marbles or small rocks. Hang bats, ghosts, Spanish moss, spiders, and webs on branch.

fall bucket

Sponge-paint outside of premade papier maché box with several fall colors of acrylic paint. Randomly adhere cut-out paper leaves to sides and lid with decoupage medium. Let dry. Apply another coat of decoupage medium. Let dry. Use box throughout the month to hold Halloween treats. After the holiday is over, it is sturdy enough to store breakable decorations.

Spooky containers can be used to decorate your home before the actual night, then transformed into trick-or-treat "bags" or treat holders to be used to hand out treats.

begging bucket

Draw a face and write the words "Thank You" on an orange plastic container, using permanent markers. Burn out marked areas with a wood-burning tool. Using craft knife, cut off spout and trim edges. Pour paint onto a paper plate. Dip sponge in paint and shade—using yellow to highlight and black to create a crusty "old" look.

23

One **haunting** night

a year,

manicured yards and

colorful flower beds are

transformed into

cold graveyards and

dismal dwelling grounds for

ghosts and *goblins*.

petrified pumpkins

Create these pumpkins for your porch and dare those teenagers to smash them in the road! Collect unusually shaped, medium-sized rocks. Wash dirt off and let dry. Epoxy rocks together, using little ones for eyes, feet, mouths, and noses. Let epoxy set. Gesso the entire creation to make a base for the paint. Let dry.

Refer to the Pumpkin Patch on page 28 for face ideas. Using acrylic paints, color the stems green, the mouths red, and the eyes white and yellow. Trim pumpkins with curled pipe cleaners and silk leaves. Do not be spooked—they are only rocks!

26

prancing pumpkins

Refer to the Pumpkin Patch on page 28 for face ideas. Lightly draw faces on concave sides of orange Styrofoam® plates. Using a paper punch, make holes at the top and bottom of each plate. Tie a 12" piece of black ribbon between plates. String 5–6 plates together. Tie a loop at the top for hanging and tie some ribbon strands through the hole on the bottom plate. Hang plate strands in the wind, causing them to flutter and prance.

PUMPKIN PATCH

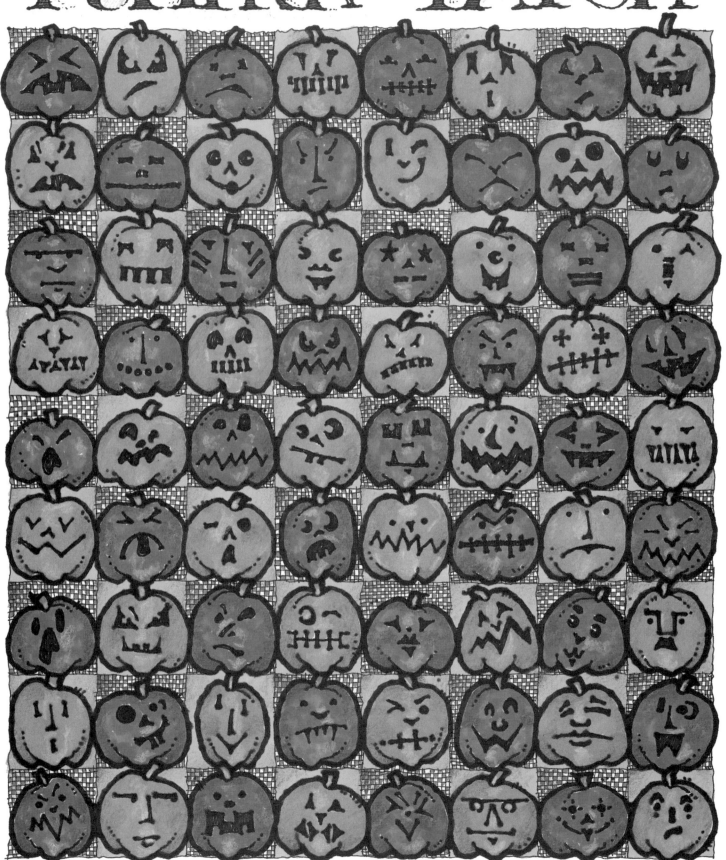

melted witch

Lay black cloth in a heap on the ground. Place witch's hat on top of heap. Stuff striped socks with newspaper and place in pointy shoes. Place socks under fabric like they are just snaking out, ready to trip anyone who passes too close. Burn the straw tips of an old broom. Cut or break the handle end off to about 2½'. Set a bucket on its side next to the heap. A piece or two of dry ice under the hat brim will add the final touch.

The witch pictured below has melted in front of a decorative sculpture.

Sculpture by Brent Mooney

Materials	
Batting	Knee socks, 1 pair
Embroidery needle	Pom-poms, 3mm
& floss	Ribbon
Hemp cord, 1 yd	Scissors

hangman

Cut knee sock at ankle. Cut cuff in half lengthwise. Roll and stitch for legs. Cut end of toe and heel from foot of sock and discard. Attach legs to foot of sock, then stuff body. Gather neck about 1" down from top opening. Tightly wrap thread around neck, making it about ¼" long. Stuff head tightly. Gather top. Tuck top in and stitch.

Make arms 5" long from other sock. Cut, roll, and stitch like legs. Wrap thread around wrists ¾" from end. Stitch arms to shoulders.

Refer to How to Stitch on page 93. Stitch pom-poms onto head for eyes. Cross-stitch over eyes. Embroider nose and mouth with tongue hanging out. Tie ribbon around waist. Refer to Hangman's Noose on page 31. Tie noose with hemp. Hang man where he can swing and sway in the wind.

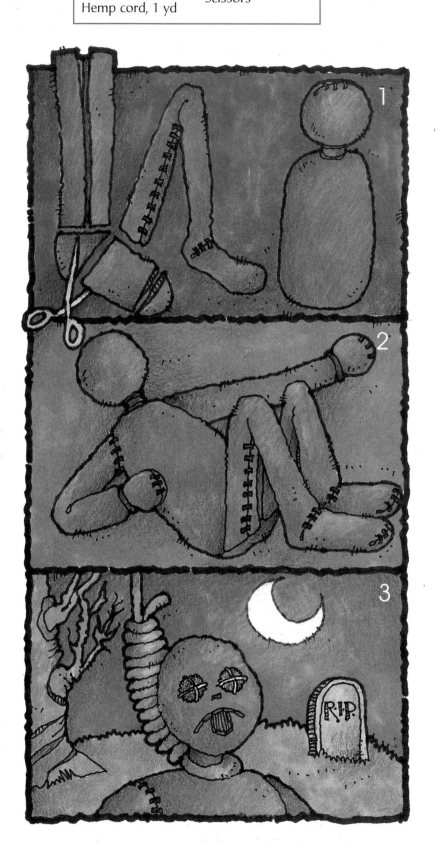

hangman's noose

Make loop desired size, leaving a long end. Wrap working end seven times counterclockwise. Bring end through top loop (eye) and pull bottom loop tight.

Tighten turns one at a time. Finish at eye.

Pull eye of knot down and slide turns left. Check that noose runs freely.

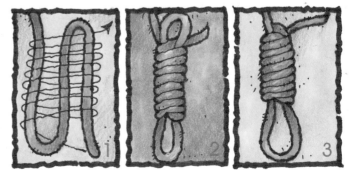

scary tip:

Take a minute and think about scary things. It is not unlike hidden pictures. You think you see a complete picture; however with closer scrutiny, there are many hidden details. From one quick look, all is well and fine; but with a closer look, you see details that surprise, amaze, and sometimes shock. That is part of the magic of Halloween. Place surprises everywhere, and do not forget the yard or porch.

Look through your old junk for interesting articles. Take a walk around your home and see if these things can be hidden, tucked away, or disguised somewhere. Bird cages filled with candles, toy cars hanging from bare tree branches, plastic dolls sitting on fences, brushes growing from the garden—all bring interest and surprise to your yard.

While planting your surprises, make up stories to go with them so you will have something to tell the children and neighbors—maybe to spark their imaginations.

Tuck interesting objects in unusual places around your house and yard. This may entail bringing outdoor things in or indoor things out. Simply keep the element of surprise in mind.

chameleon

Materials	
Batting	Needle & thread
Embellishments:	Pins
sequins, pearl beads	Scissors
Green velvet, 1 yd	Sewing machine

Using Chameleon patterns on page 35, cut out velvet. Sew arms and legs. Clip, turn, and stuff with batting. Stitch through knees and elbows to make them bend.

Sew insert into tummy, from chest to base of tail. Leave top of head open for turning. Sew darts. Clip and turn. Stuff tail tightly. Stuff body, neck, then head.

Sew, clip, and turn crown. Stuff lightly and sew into top of head opening. Sew mouth and inside mouth pieces together. Clip, turn, and stuff. Refer to How to Stitch on page 93. Make running stitch around lip and stitch mouth onto head. Gather-stitch around edges of cheek cir-cles. Stuff and stitch cheeks above corners of mouth.

Fold eye circle in half and sew ⅛" from fold. Fold in half opposite and sew again. Fold in quarters, then eights, and so forth until each eye is fanned. Gather-stitch around edges of eyes. Stuff and stitch eyes onto head. Pinch nose and stitch through to make nostrils. Bead with gold, green, pearl, and silver sequins. Cover any flaws or mistakes with beads.

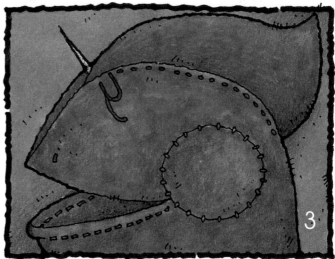

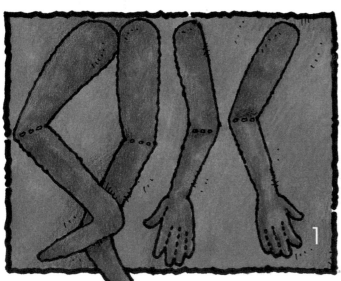

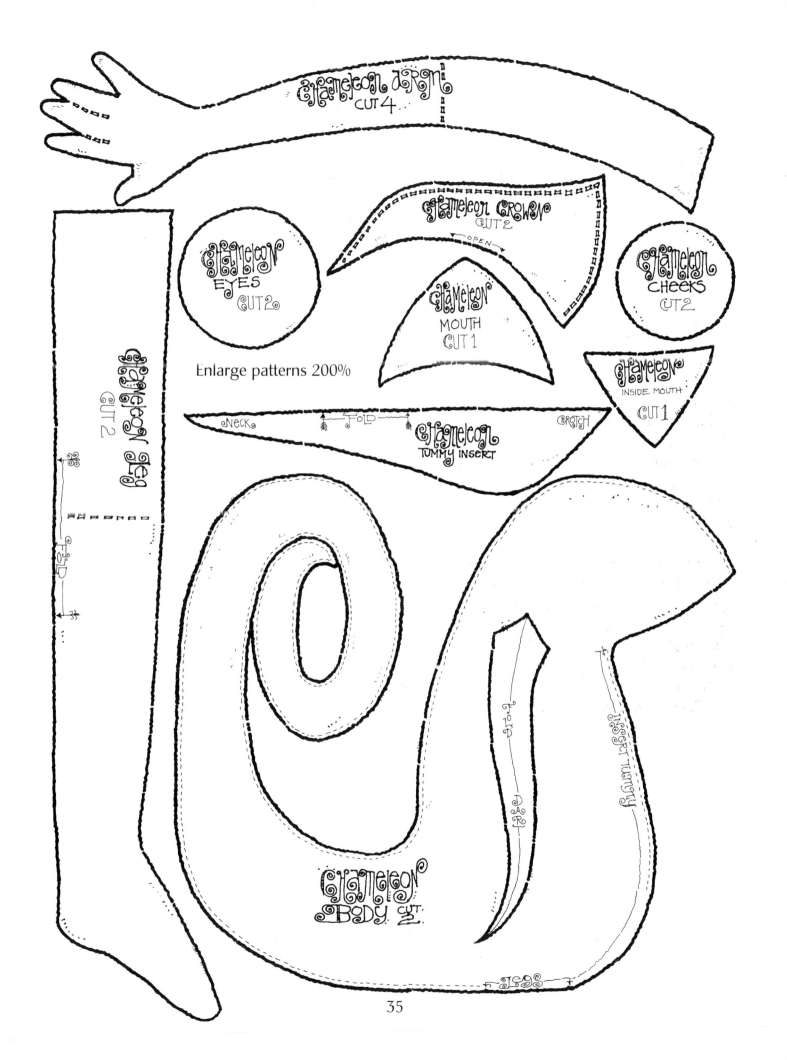

Chameleon Arm
CUT 4

Chameleon Crown
CUT 2
OPEN

Chameleon Eyes
CUT 2

Chameleon Cheeks
CUT 2

Chameleon Mouth
CUT 1

Chameleon Inside Mouth
CUT 1

Enlarge patterns 200%

Chameleon Leg
CUT 2

NECK   FOLD   CROTCH
Chameleon Tummy Insert

FOLD DART

INSERT TUMMY

Chameleon Body CUT 2

LEG

35

owl lantern

Materials
Acrylic paints: black, clear, yellow
Brown paper
Cardboard
Card stock
Masking tape
Paintbrushes
Papier maché body (page 92)
Scissors
Small flashlight

Make paper cones for beak, horns, and wings. Tape beak, horns, and wings to body, keeping opening at bottom.

Cut a 3"-diameter cardboard circle. Cut feet from circle. Cut strip from card stock for base. Roll to fit opening and tape ends together. Tape base to feet.

Tear brown paper into 2" squares. Mix more papier maché paste and cover entire owl and base with brown paper. For eyes, crinkle wet paper into balls and adhere onto owl's face. Let dry. Paint eyes, then feather pattern on body and wings with acrylic paints. Let dry. Coat entire owl with clear acrylic. Place flashlight in base and set body over base.

bat-a-bat piñata

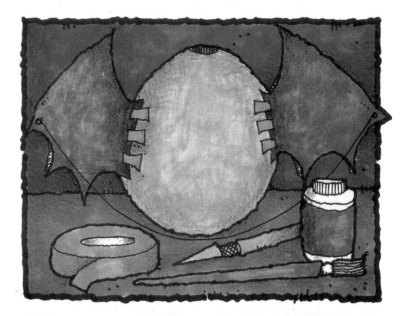

Cut two wings from cardboard. Cut 1" slits into edge of wings that will go next to body. Turn body upside-down and tape wings in place. Poke holes in tip of wings to string fish line for hanging.

Paint entire bat black. Cut table tennis ball in half and hot-glue to body for eyes. Paint red dots on eyes and a black dot in center for dilated pupil. Paint white pointy teeth. Add drops of blood down chin with red.

Place small toys and wrapped candy in red tulle squares, then secure bundles with ribbon. Place bundles in body and seal with tape to create piñata. Hang piñata low enough for child to hit with stick. Let blind-folded children take turns hitting the piñata to break it open.

SCARY TIP:
Refer to How to Make Foreboding Dough on page 93 to create Dough Bats (right). String together with ribbon and hang conspicuously around your yard.

B e **aware** of the interior

of a home.

Haunted corners and

darkened halls beckon to

grab you into their clutches.

Witches and *ghosts* lurk

in every room, while ghouls

move *swiftly* about. Either join the

force or be spooked the whole

season long.

insane inside

ghostower

Paint terra-cotta pot black. Let dry. Hot-glue circle of felt onto bottom to avoid marring furniture. Cut a ghost shape from sponge. Pour white paint onto paper plate. Daub sponge in white paint and press against pot. Move sponge around to make image fuzzy and hazy. Let dry. Fill bottom of pot with crumpled newspaper. If cone is smaller than pot opening, glue cone to paper plate and cut plate to fit opening.

Tear twenty 5" squares from gray or white fabric. Randomly adhere over cone and glue in place. The edges look old when left raggedy and rough. Tear strips from Halloween print or cheesecloth and wrap around cone. Hot-glue in place. Thread sequin onto pins and push into cone to catch light. Tie knots and tuck fabric into pot.

One ghost will need one 8" square each of cheesecloth and tulle. Place pom-pom next to Styrofoam ball for head and chin. Cover both with facial tissue. Cover head with cheesecloth then tulle. It will look more layered and dimensional if fabrics do not match up. Wrap 9" length of ribbon around neck twice and tie under chin. Do not trim excess. Push pin into concave side of sequin, then into head for eye. Repeat for other eye. Pin and glue ghosts around cone, positioning them as if spiraling upward. Use plenty of pins in sequins to secure fabric out, around, and overlapping. Make extra ghosts to arrange on curtains.

Materials
Acrylic paints: black, white
Cheesecloth, 2 pkg
Craft knife
Fabrics: Halloween print, ¼ yd
    gray or white scraps
    white tulle lace, 2 yd
Felt
Hot-glue gun & glue sticks
Newspaper
Paper plates
Sponge
Styrofoam® balls, 1½" (10–15)
Styrofoam® cone
Terra-cotta pot
White facial tissue
White pom-poms (10–15)
White ribbon
White round-headed pins
White sequins

Materials
Bonded batting
Buttons, 2–4 holes
Halloween-print fabrics, 15" x 2 yd
   (2 coordinating)
Iron & ironing board
Pins
Ribbons: black, green, orange
Scissors
Sewing machine & thread

table Runner

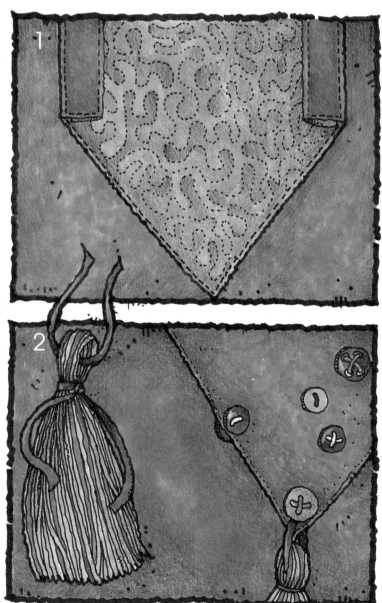

Tear 15" from each Halloween print. Fold in half, with right sides together. Cut 8"-long points on all four ends. Cut 16" x 2 yard piece of batting. Pin to both pieces (still right sides together) and sew around ½" from edge, leaving a 5" hole for turning. Trim off excess, turn, and press. Topstitch outside edges. Randomly quilt-stitch top if desired. Fold edges over 1" and sew for border and top.

Stitch buttons on both sides of points to act as weights. Make tassels from fourteen 5" ribbons folded in half and secure with ribbon in center. Tightly tie another piece of ribbon about 1" down. Stitch to points of table runner with buttons on each side.

masked funeral wreath

spooky spider

Materials
Black quilting thread
Chenille stems: black bumpy (4), sparkly (5)
Needle
Pom-poms: black, 1" (2), 1½", 2"; red 3mm (2)

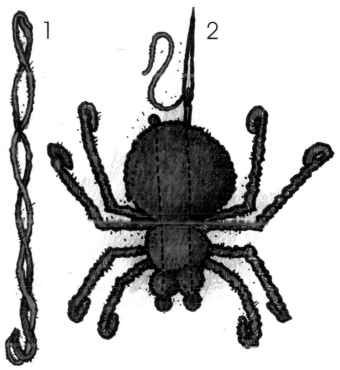

Cover work space with newspaper. Wrap 2"-wide ribbon around grapevine wreath until covered. Push ends into grapevine and hot-glue in place. Tie ribbon at top for hanging. Push silk leaves up stem to base of flower, then cut stem 2"–4" long. Place flowers between vines and bend wire stem around vine. Group different shapes, sizes, and textures together. Cover most of front of wreath.

Remove elastic from masks and replace with 12"–15" lengths of ½"-wide ribbon. Place masks on front of wreath, then wrap ribbon around to back and knot in front. Leave ribbons hanging.

Push branches into wreath and hot-glue in place inside and outside wreath. Spray-paint entire wreath, angling spray to shade certain areas. Let dry. Hot-glue spiders onto wreath. Randomly, spread spider webs around wreath.

Twist together one sparkly and one bumpy chenille stem. Bend each end over 1" to form feet. Fold in half to make two legs. Repeat three more times. Bend legs in center to form knees.

Push needle and thread through 2" pom-pom for abdomen. Pull taut, hiding knot, then wrap thread around two sets of legs, securing to abdomen. Be certain legs are secure. Push needle through 1½" pom-pom and secure two more legs to body. Push needle up through body and secure one 1" black and one red pom-pom for eye. Repeat for remaining eye. Push needle and thread through body and abdomen. Tie knot where web would come out and leave thread long to tie to wreath.

jack's lantern

Fill metal can with water ¼" from top and freeze to maintain can shape. Draw simple shapes and designs on paper and tape to can. Place can on towel folded into fourths. Using hammer and large nail, punch holes through can and into ice along lines. Big holes are best. Refreeze if ice starts to melt.

grimmaracas

Materials
Acrylic paints:
    black, clear, red
Masking tape
Paintbrushes

Papier maché
    grimmaracas (2) (page 92)
Rice or beans
Sticks, 12" long (2)
White paper

Place 2–3 table-spoons of rice or beans inside each grimmaraca. Insert stick into each open-ing and tape in place, leaving most of stick out for handle.

Mix more paste and cover grimmaracas and sticks with torn white paper. Do not get them too wet or they will cave in. Let dry.

Refer to faces from Skull Banner on page 18. Paint skeleton faces on grimmaracas. Cover with clear acrylic. Let dry.

spoon spectors

Materials
Acrylic paints: black, ivory, red
Chenille stems: black, white
Craft glue
Drill & 1/8" drill bit
Gesso
Fabric scraps: black, gray, print, white
Fabrics: black print, 1/4 yd
  white print, 1/4 yd
Needle & crochet thread
Paintbrushes
Pins
Ribbons and trims
Scissors
Wooden spoons
Yarns: black, white

Drill hole through neck of spoon for arm placement. Gesso, then paint spoons with ivory paint. Using Spoon Spectors face patterns on page 53, paint faces on back side of spoons with black and a bit of red. Slide two chenille stems through predrilled hole and center for arms. Twist ends to form hands. Tear 1" x 22" strips of black fabric for sleeves and white fabric for hands. Fray edges. Wrap around chenille stems and glue in place. Secure with pins until dry. Be certain to keep thumbs up.

Tear 3" x 12" pieces from black and white prints and plain fabrics for capes, dresses, and other clothing. For collars, fold fabric down 1". Refer to How to Stitch on page 93. Using running stitch, gather along raw edge with crochet thread. Tightly gather around neck. Cut a small hole in each side of cape for arms to go through and stitch sleeves to cape. Glue cape at neck, then tie with ribbon or string.

Wrap chenille stems into ringlets and adhere to head for hair, or simply paint on hair. Bride's hair is 6" lengths of black and white yarns glued on toward face, then pulled back around entire edge of spoon. Tie into ponytail and trim.

SPOOK SPECTERS

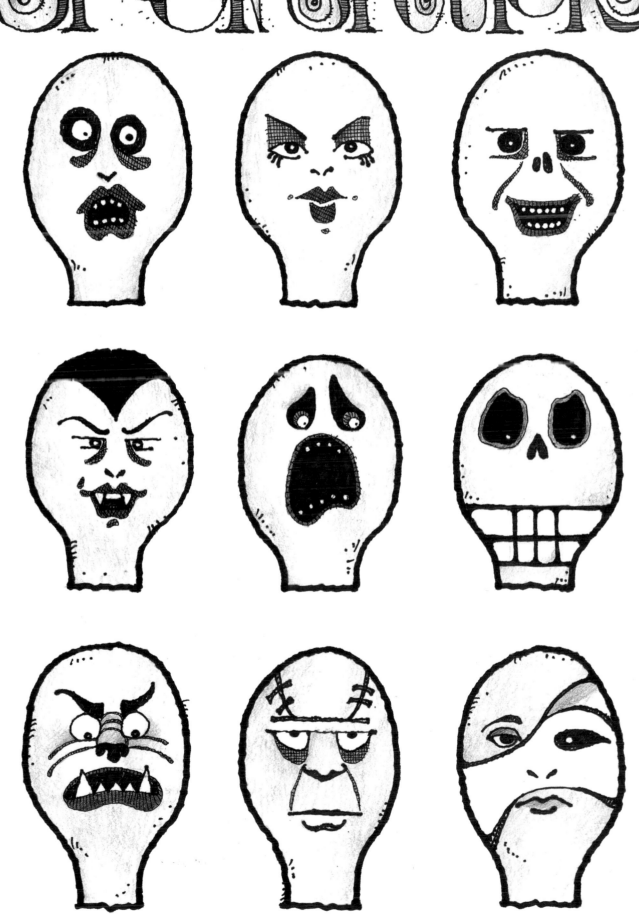

burial chamber chair

Materials
Fabrics: grassy print, 5" x 40"
    Halloween print
    patterned strips, 1" x 18"
    unbleached muslin, 23" x 40"
Fusible bonding
Iron & ironing board
Scissors
Sewing machine & thread

Tear two 20" x 23" pieces from muslin for each chair. Sew pieces together for tombstone chair cover, leaving bottom open. Turn right side out and press. Find center of grassy print and stitch onto front center of tombstone.

Tear 1" x 20" strip of patterned fabric and sew one end of each strip to each bottom corner of grassy strip with right sides together. These ties will go on back side of chair.

Refer to Letters & Numbers on page 94. Transfer and cut desired letters from fusible bonding. Fuse letters onto Halloween prints and cut out. Fuse Halloween-print letters onto back of tombstone. Place cover over chairs.

HOW MUCH DIRT IS IN A GRAVE HOLE?

NONE, A HOLE IS EMPTY.

S ometimes

we enjoy the

Halloween holiday more than others.

We can't wait to let the

ghosts and goblins rise up

from the *cellar*.

We entice the witch off the roof

and the goblin out of the closet

to adorn our house

all month long.

all month long

Materials
Assorted small toys or
    wrapped candy
Batting, ½ yd
Black fleece, 17" x 11"
Clear-drying glue
¾" Dowel
Embellishments: beads,
    buttons, pom-poms
Felt: coordinating colors
Halloween fabrics:
    large print, 1 yd
    small print, ¼ yd
Velcro®: hook side only
Iron & ironing board
Iron-on fusing
Iron-on patch fabrics:
    black, white
Large pom-poms: black,
    green, orange
Needle & crochet thread
Pins
Ribbons: black, green,
    orange, purple
Scissors
Sewing machine

panicalendar

Tear large print fabric in half, making rectangle approximately 23" x 36". With right sides together, pin batting to wrong side of fabric and sew long sides and bottom. Clip corners and edges. Turn and press. Tear and fray six 2" x 18" strips of small print fabric for pockets. Place and pin strips of fabric approximately 2" from bottom, and ¾" apart. Last strip will be 15" from bottom of calendar. Stitch ½" in from bottom and sides of strips. Stitch through strips every 2½" for each pocket. The pockets should open at top. Glue black fleece in place above pockets. Refer to How to Stitch on page 93. Blanket-stitch around border of fleece with crochet thread.

Fold top edges over 2" toward front for rod pocket. Tuck raw edges under ½" and hand-stitch in place. Sew ribbon onto hand-stitched edge as desired. Insert dowel through rod pocket. Tie several lengths of ribbon to dowel ends. Glue large black, green, and orange pom-poms onto dowel ends.

Using Letters & Numbers patterns on page 94, cut out numbers 1–30 from iron-on patch fabrics. Alternate between black and white. Cut out twelve white ghosts and their black eyes to be ironed onto end pockets of six strips. Position numbers and ghosts and press in place. Add beads, buttons, and pom-poms.

Glue two pieces of felt together for more stability. Cut out letters from orange felt. Using examples on page 60, cut out shapes from assorted felt colors. Refer to How to Stitch on page 93. Blanket-stitch around edges and stitch details into front of shapes. Sew or glue Velcro to back of each shape. Cut picket fence from white patch fabric and iron onto black fleece for picture background. Place candy, felt cutouts, and small toys in pockets. Remove the corresponding article each day. If it is a felt figure, add it to picture background.

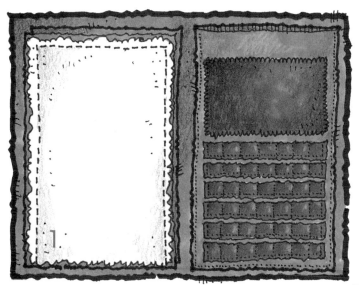

SPOOKY SYMBOLS & CHARMS

THE CROW & HIS BROTHER THE RAVEN ARE SEEN AS ILL OMENS, SIGN OF WAR, ILLNESS OR DEATH. A BLACK FEATHER MEANS DEATH TO AN ENEMY.

THE NEWT IS A MAIN INGREDIENT IN WITCHES' BREW. IT WILL CONJURE UP EVIL SPIRITS TO REVEAL THE FUTURE.

POINTED WITCH'S HAT SYMBOLIZES CONE OF POWER

CHARMS OF ALL KINDS ARE WORN AS PROTECTION FROM ILLNESS OR DANGER—GLASS EYE, TO TURN AWAY EVIL EYE—FOUR LEAF CLOVER OR HORSESHOE ARE CHARMS OF GOOD LUCK—TOADS REPEL POISON—CRYSTALS FOR HEALING—DICE ARE SYMBOLS FOR UNPREDICTABLE LUCK—AND A STAR BRINGS LIGHT INTO DARK.

A FIVE-POINTED STAR UPSIDE DOWN IS AN EVIL SYMBOL. A RIGHT SIDE UP STAR IS A SYMBOL FOR LIGHT AND WAS PAINTED ON HOUSES FOR PROTECTION AGAINST WITCHES.

WITCHES RIDE BROOMS. THIS IS ASSOCIATED WITH FERTILE HARVESTS.

LONG AGO IT WAS BELIEVED WITCHES TURNED THEMSELVES INTO BLACK CATS. SOME BELIEVE BLACK CATS SCARE AWAY THE THINGS THAT GO BUMP IN THE DARK, OR IF A BLACK CAT CROSSES YOUR PATH, THE DEVIL IS THINKING ABOUT YOU.

ANGELS ARE A GOOD OR BAD SYMBOL OF THE GO-BETWEEN FOR SOULS BETWEEN LIFE AND DEATH.

LONG AGO IT WAS BELIEVED WITCHES WERE IN LEAGUE WITH THE DEVIL, BREWED MAGIC POTIONS, AND CAST SPELLS. WOMEN HEALERS WERE BRANDED AS EVIL AND IN THE 1700S, PUT TO DEATH.

61

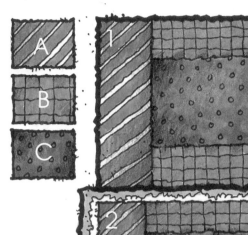

peek-a-boo quilt

Machine-stitch fabric pieces A, B, and C together with ½" seams. Press.

Place batting on wrong side of quilt back. Center quilt top on batting, leaving enough fabric around edges so quilt back can be folded over quilt front with a 1" border.

Using needle and quilting thread, hand-quilt in ditches along seam lines. Hand-stitch outside border.

Refer to Letters & Numbers on page 94. Cut the letters BOO from white flannel. Pin and hand-stitch letters in place about ¼" from edge on quilt top. Use and washings will fray edges.

Refer to How to Stitch on page 93. Using blanket-stitch, tack border around edges. Finish quilt around and inside letters with buttons and orange ribbon.

wolf feet

Glue false fingernails onto furry toe socks. Enjoy the clicking of your toes on the floor as you welcome trick-or-treaters.

halloween store-all

Cover cardboard box with brown paper. Tear four pumpkin shapes from orange construction paper. Apply decoupage medium to adhere a pumpkin to each side of box. Apply decoupage medium to entire box. Tie up box with hemp when full of Halloween decorations.

ghastly tassel

Materials
All-purpose glue
Carpet needle
Foreboding dough
  (page 93)
Knitting needle
Oven
Paintbrush, small
Red pom-poms, 3mm (2)
Scissors
Shot glass
Strong string
Video-tape-sized box
White paint
Yarns: black, gray, natural,
  off-white, silver, white

1 Pinch off and flatten out golf-ball-sized pieces of dough. Using moistened fingers, scallop edges. Place over shot glass. Poke hole in top with knitting needle. Bake at 350°F until dry.

2 Paint ghoul white. Glue red pom-poms on for eyes.

3 Wrap yarn around box widthwise approximately 20 times. Use black, gray, natural, off-white, or silver for mixing colors. Tightly tie string at top, leaving tails. Clip bottom loops.

4 Thread tails up through hole in ghoul. Double-knot and secure with glue.

soapy spooks

Materials

Batting
Craft glue
Hand towels, 11" x 18" (3)
Iron & ironing board
Needle & quilting thread
Red fabric
Red iron-on tape
Scissors
Tiny pom-poms: black, red, white
Washcloths

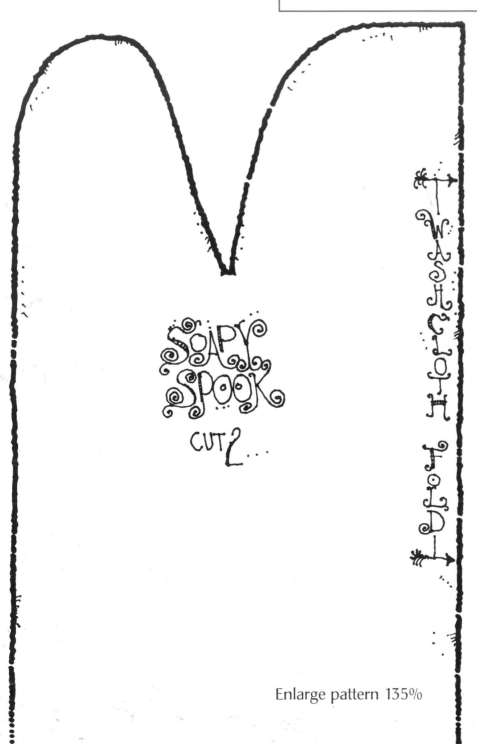

SOAPY SPOOK

CUT 2...

WASHCLOTH FOLD

Enlarge pattern 135%

Fold washcloth in half. Cut off corners to round-off top. With right sides together, sew up side and top for body. Turn right side out. Cut facial features from iron-on tape. Press in place. Adhere pom-poms for teeth.

Cut one hand towel in half for arms. Roll sides to middle and stitch. Keep fringe on bottom for hands. Sew on arms. Sew two hand towels together. Turn inside out for body. Gather 1"–2" down from top with quilting thread for hair. Place marble-sized ball of batting inside head. Stitch around batting to form nose. Glue pom-poms above nose for eyes. Cut mouth from red fabric and stitch to face.

Fold washcloth into triangle. Sew up one side. Turn inside out. Decorate with iron-on tape and pom-poms.

Place two washcloths together and fold in half. Using Soapy Spook pattern on page 66, cut V's from top, making head (on fold) and two arms. Sew along sides and top, leaving bottom open and turn inside out. Use pom-poms for eyes and nose. Cut oval from iron-on tape for mouth. Cut mouth into two pieces with jagged line. Separate and press in place.

SCARY THINGS

ORIGINALLY, THE SCARECROW WAS PUT IN THE FIELD TO PROTECT CROPS FROM FAILING. NOT FOR A BIRD PERCH.

THE MOON HOLDS ALOT OF INFLUENCE OVER CREATURES OF THE NIGHT—BATS, OWLS, CATS, AND WOLVES. THE LATIN WORD FOR MOON IS LUNA. LUNATIC MEANS "MOONSTRUCK".

TO SOME, THE CRY OF AN OWL MEANS BAD LUCK OR DEATH. IT IS ASSOCIATED WITH THE NIGHT—WHICH CAN BE SCARY.

THE REFLECTION OF A MIRROR MEANS TRUTH, CLARITY & SELF-KNOWLEDGE. THUS A BROKEN MIRROR MEANS BAD LUCK TO ONESELF.

THE SKELETON IS THE SYMBOL OF DEATH. IT IS OFTEN SHOWN CARRYING A SCYTHE OR HOURGLASS AS A REMINDER OF THE SPEEDY PASSING OF TIME.

WE COVER OUR MOUTHS WHEN YAWNING TO KEEP DEMONS FROM JUMPING DOWN OUR THROATS AND STEALING OUR SOULS.
WE KNOCK ON WOOD AFTER A HOPEFUL STATEMENT BECAUSE IN OLDEN DAYS IT WAS BELIEVED HARMFUL SPIRITS LIVED IN HOLLOW TREES. THEY RUIN OVER-HEARD PLANS, BUT KNOCKING SCARES THEM AWAY.
WHEN WE SHAKE HANDS, IT'S SHOWING THAT NEITHER PERSON IS CARRYING A WEAPON.
OVER THE CENTURIES "GOD BE WITH YE" HAS BECOME "GOOD 'BYE."

THE SKULL SYMBOLIZES DEATH, DANGER, AND HOW TEMPORARY LIFE IS. THE SKULL-&-CROSSBONES WERE AN EVIL WARNING OF THE PIRATES-SIGNAL TO ALL WHO SAW IT— DEATH!

voodoo doll

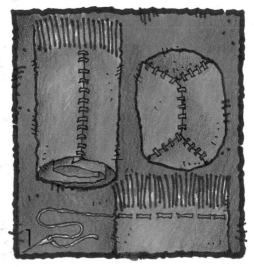
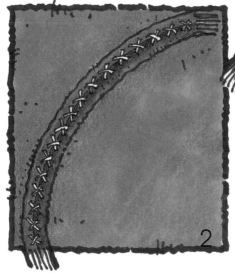
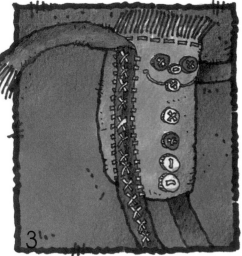

Fray light burlap along one long edge approximately 3" down. (This will be the hair.) Roll up burlap to make 6" x 19" body. Tuck in and stitch up back edge. Stuff slightly with batting. Box-fold bottom like a gift and stitch shut. Refer to How to Stitch on page 93. Using large running stitch-es, sew head shut below frayed edge.

Fray all short edges of dark burlap and roll up each piece lengthwise. Tuck in long edges and cross-stitch shut for arms and legs.

Making arm 12", stitch dark burlap along side of body. Repeat for other side. Dark burlap will extend below body to form legs. Stitch arms down so they do not stick straight up. Embellish front and form facial features with buttons and crochet thread.

> **Materials**
> Batting
> Burlap: light, 19" x 48"
>   dark, 9" x 40" (2)
> Buttons
> Needle & crochet thread
> Scissors

Legend claimed that if a wicked witch was given a piece of hair or even a toenail clipping, she could use it to make a fetish. By putting pins into it, she could cause pain in different parts of the owner's body.

With outstretched arms and *puppy dog eyes*,

we display monsters

that may appear *tender* and

inviting. However, let

these **monsters** get too close

and you will find a creepy,

cold **grasp** only

creatures can share.

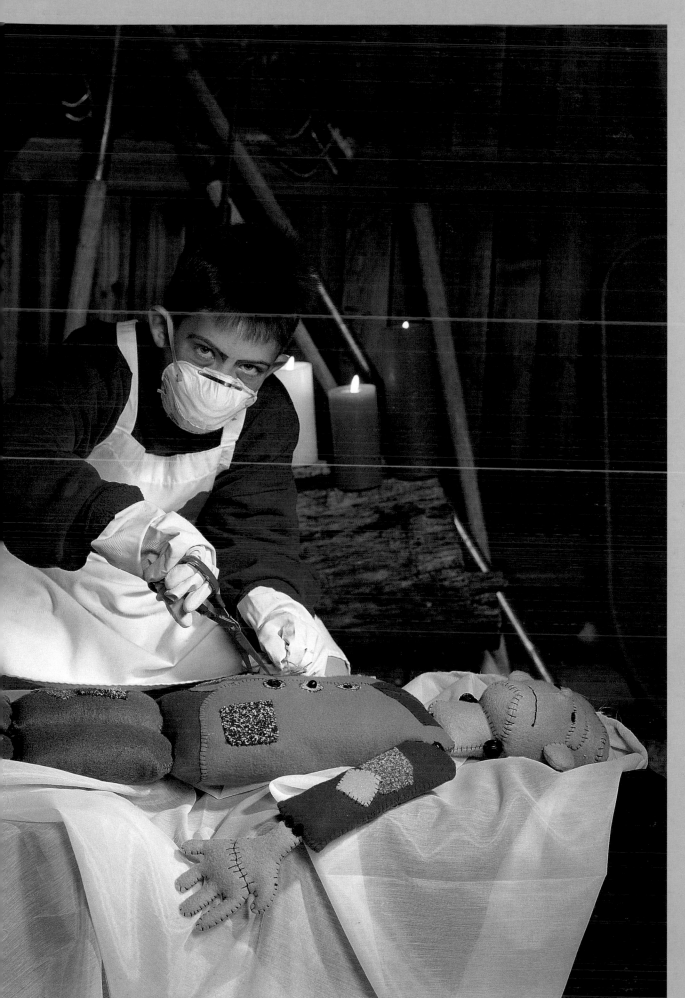

monster mayhem

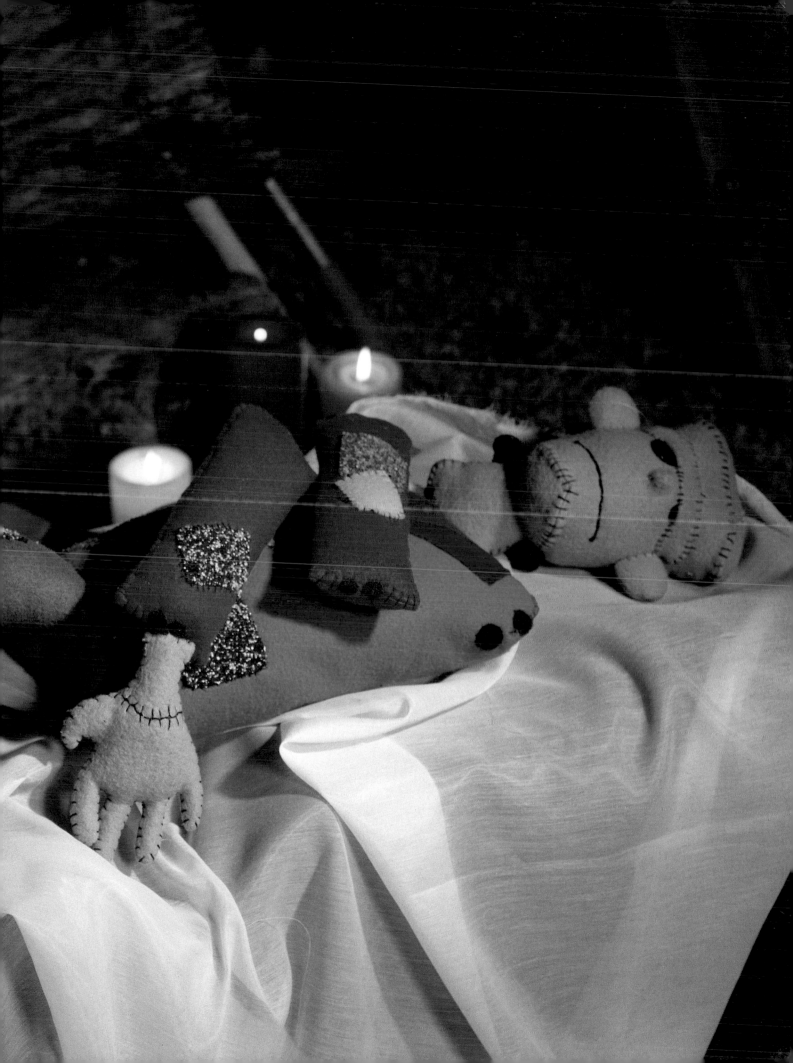

Frank's Monster

Materials
Batting
Black buttons
Black crochet thread
Fabric scraps
Fleece ½ yd each: lime green, olive green, orange, reversible turquoise
Needle & thread
Photocopier
Round Velcro® patches:
   ½" sets (14)
Scissors
Sewing machine

Enlarge and cut out Frank's Monster pattern pieces on pages 78–79. Refer to How to Stitch on page 93. Cut and sew the following body parts from lime green fleece:

Arms: Cut two 6" x 9" pieces. Fold each piece in half with right sides together. Using large stitches, close up 9" sides.

Calves: Cut two 8" x 9" pieces. Fold each piece in half with right sides together. Using large stitches, close up 9" sides.

Thighs: Cut two 7" x 8" pieces. Fold each piece in half with right sides together. Tuck top corners in ½". Using large stitches, close up 7" sides.

Turn all body parts right side out. Stuff, then stitch each part closed. Cut, then stitch on a variety of patches with large stitches.

Using sewing machine and ½" seams, sew up hands, then clip and turn. Stuff, then stitch wrists closed. Topstitch across palms of hands.

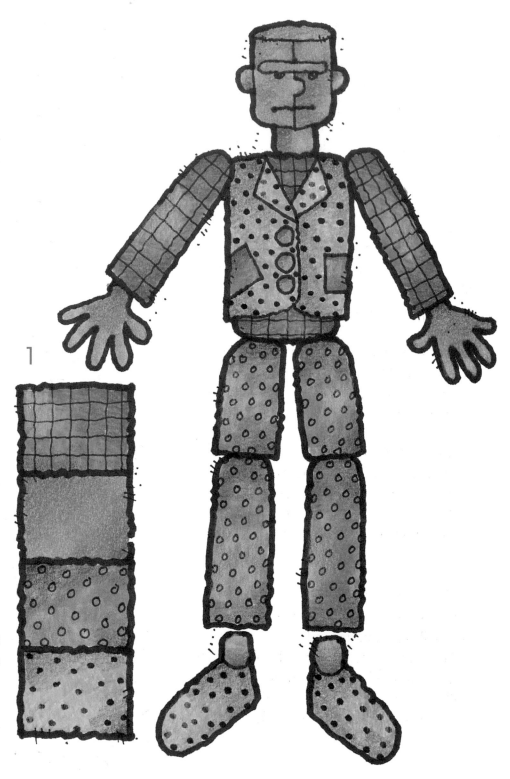

1

To make jacket, fold 20" x 13" piece of turquoise fleece in half (10" x 13") and curve bottom corners. Fold top corners down to make lapels and stitch in place. One side will overlap the other 1". Cut two pieces from orange fleece, one 6½" x 8" for shirt and one 8" x 9" for waist. Fold shirt in half with wrong sides together. Place inside jacket, with fold at top, and blanket-stitch around neckline of jacket. Fold waist piece in half and stitch up sides. Place inside jacket, with fold extending 1" from bottom of jacket, and blanket-stitch around bottom of jacket. Stuff body and stitch jacket front shut. Sew on three or four buttons and contrasting patches.

To make head, use sewing machine to sew along profile. Sew chin gusset in place. Sew oval piece onto top of head. Clip and turn. Stuff and stitch around oval. Sew, turn, and stuff ears. Stitch ears to sides of head. Stitch eyebrow across forehead. Make "stitches" under chin and anywhere else desired. Straight-stitch mouth with French knots in corners. Sew buttons under eyebrow for eyes and on neck for bolts.

Cut shoes from olive green fleece. Stitch top to sole and stuff. Topstitch around sole with crochet thread. Cut two 2½" x 7" ankles. Fold in half and stitch into stuffed shoe. Stitch Velcro circles onto top and bottom of each body piece. Alternate the hook and loop sides so there is only one way to put him together.

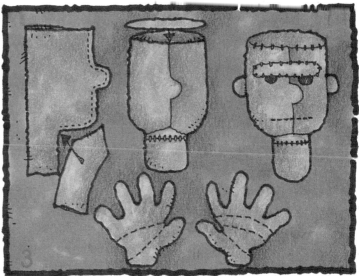

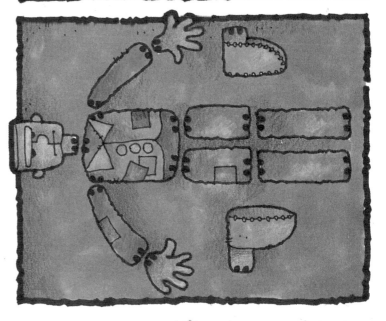

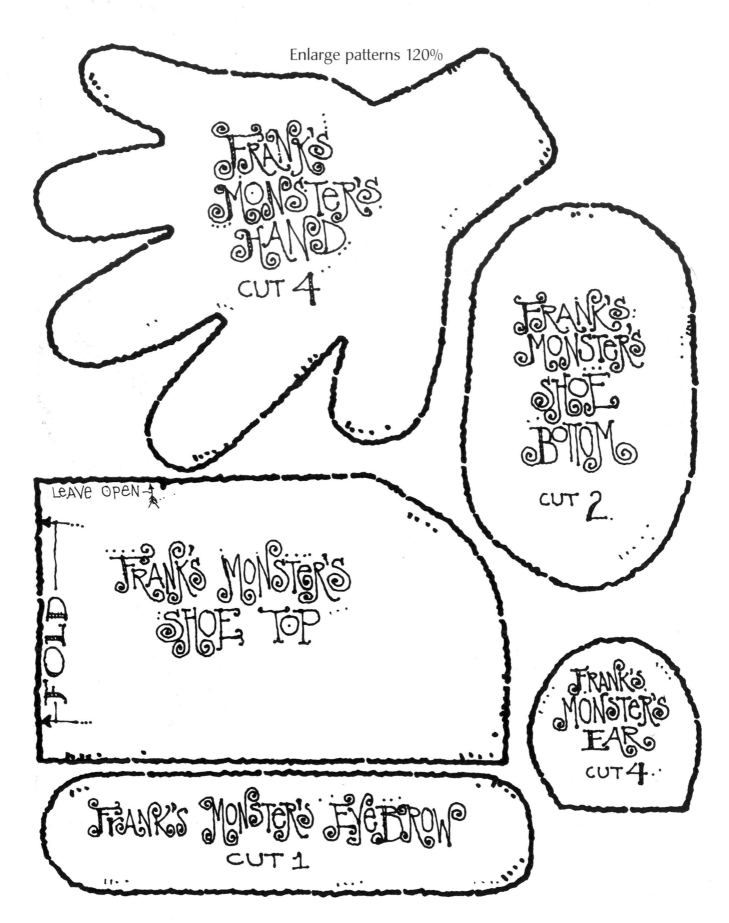

Enlarge patterns 120%

FRANK'S MONSTER'S HAND
CUT 4

FRANK'S MONSTER'S SHOE BOTTOM
CUT 2

LEAVE OPEN

FOLD

FRANK'S MONSTER'S SHOE TOP

FRANK'S MONSTER'S EAR
CUT 4

FRANK'S MONSTER'S EYEBROW
CUT 1

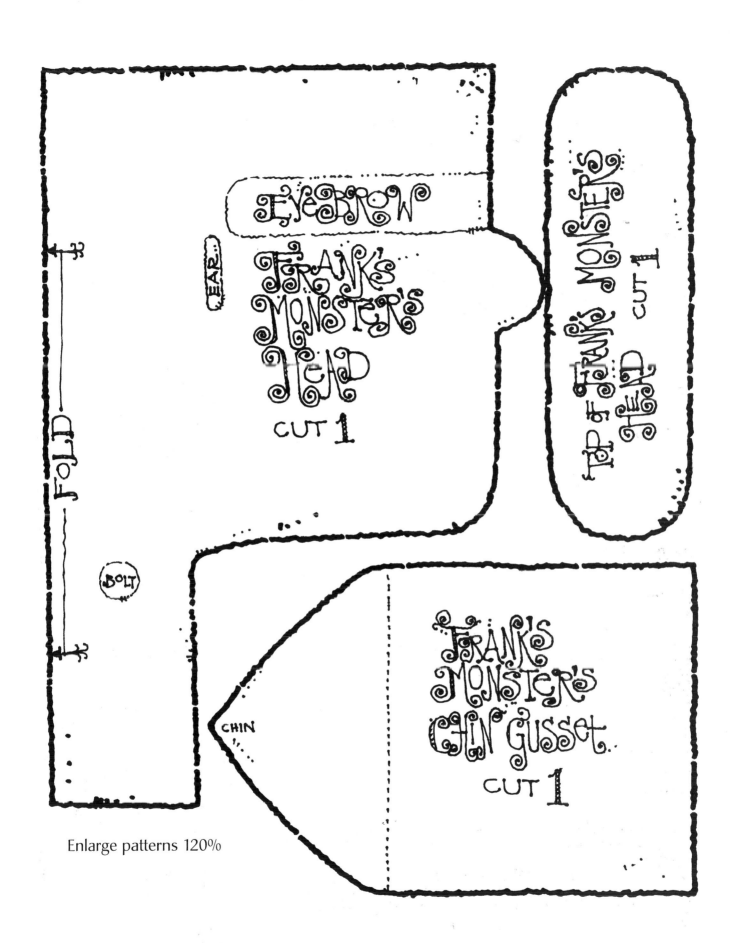

FOLD

BOLT

EYEBROW

EAR

FRANK'S MONSTER'S HEAD
CUT 1

TOP of FRANK'S MONSTER'S HEAD CUT 1

CHIN

FRANK'S MONSTER'S CHIN GUSSET
CUT 1

Enlarge patterns 120%

79

mummy man

Remove two beads from back of one armature. Add three beads to each arm and four beads to each leg. Cover entire body with batting, securing with thread.

Make two hands, with thumbs and fingers, from wire. Wind wire around wrist bead. Place batting in center of hand, securing with thread.

Make a wad of batting a little smaller than a table tennis ball, securing to neck with thread. Form wire feet and secure to ankle bead. Cut two feet bottoms from card stock. Cover with batting, securing with thread. Tear 1"–1½" strips of muslin and fray at least ¼" in along edges. Begin wrapping strips at feet, legs, body, arms, hands, fingers, then head, stitching into place with colored crochet thread. Tie several strips around wrists and hands. Wrap several strips around his head, leaving places for eyes and mouth. Embroider face.

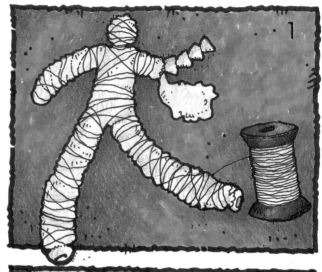

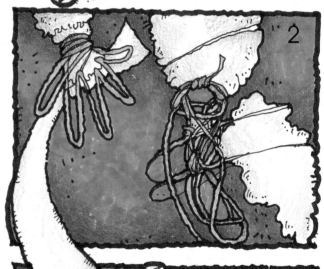

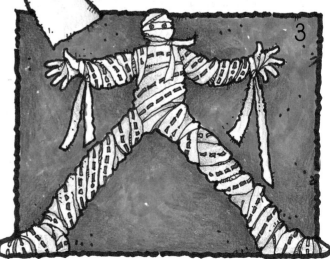

Jack was a rotten human. He beat his dog and kicked his cat. No one would come near him. He died a slow, lonely death and ended up in hell at the devil's feet. He was angry and rude to Satan, so he was sent to the outskirts of hell where he still was the epitome of rotten spirits. Soon Satan got tired of his pranks and his attitude and, after several warnings, sent him back to walk the earth for eternity. Before leaving, Jack stole a burning coal. When he reached the outside world, he found a turnip, hollowed it out, and put his burning coal in it. He discovered it did not give off enough light, so he put his glowing coal in a carved pumpkin. You can still see him wandering around— but usually on October 31.

Materials
Batting
Card stock
Crochet thread: gray, tan, yellow
Halloween-colored fleece, ½ yd
Hemp, ribbon, string, yarn
Needle
Plastic doll body armatures (2)
   (one used for parts)
Scissors
Wire

jack

Follow Steps 1 and 2 for Mummy Man on page 80. Make a wad of batting a little smaller than a table tennis ball, securing to neck with thread. Cut 3" square from fleece and center on top of head. Gather fleece around neck, adjusting folds so they are on side and back of head, leaving face flat and secure with thread. Wrap ribbon, string, and hemp around ankles, neck, and wrists for decoration. Repeat wrapping around wrists and ankles. Embroider sinister-looking face.

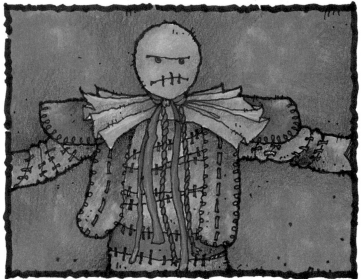

Form wire feet and secure to ankle bead. Cut two feet bottoms from card stock. Cover with batting, securing with thread. Cut 1"–1½" strips from fleece. Begin wrapping strips at feet, legs, body, arms, hands, fingers, then head, stitching along edges with colored crochet threads. Overlap colors and change thread colors often.

Cut four 1" x 2½" ovals from fleece for collar. Refer to How to Stitch on page 93. Blanket-stitch around edges. Stitch two pieces on each shoulder under fabric. Cut two 2" x 5" pieces of a different color fleece for jacket. Blanket-stitch edges together. Fold in half and place over shoulders, under collar pieces. Stitch with contrasting-colored threads.

Add desired amount of hemp, ribbon, string, or yarn to make Jack look weather-worn and creepy.

KITCH KORDS FROM MACBETH BY W. SHAKESPEARE

Round about the cauldron go; In the poison'd entrails throw. Toad, that under cold stone Days and nights has thirty-one Swelter'd venom sleeping got, Boil thou first i' the charmed pot. Double, double toil and trouble; Fire burn, and cauldron bubble. Fillet of a fenny snake, In the cauldron boil and bake; Eye of newt, and toe of frog, Wool of bat, and tongue of dog, Adder's fork, and blind-worm's sting, Lizard's leg, and howlet's wing, For a charm of powerful trouble, Like a hell-broth boil and bubble. Double, double toil and trouble; Fire burn, and cauldron bubble. Scale of dragon; tooth of wolf; Witches' mummy; maw and gulf Of the ravin'd salt-sea shark; Root of hemlock digg'd i' the dark; Liver of blaspheming Jew; Gall of goat, and slips of yew Sliver'd in the moon's eclipse; Nose of Turk, and Tartar's lips; Finger of birth-strangled babe Ditch-deliver'd by a drab—Make the gruel thick and slab: Add thereto a tiger's chaudron, For th' ingredients of our cauldron. Double, double toil and trouble; Fire burn; and, cauldron, bubble. Cool it with a baboon's blood, Then the charm is firm and good.

witch with
candy-corn knickers

Materials
Batting
Beads: black, gold, yellow
Black craft foam, 10" circle (2)
Black-headed pin
Black tulle lace, 1 yd (hat)
Black yarn
Book, 13" tall
Card stock
Cotton ball
½" Dowel, 13" long
½" Elastic
Fabrics: black, 1 yd (skirt, sleeves, top)
   black print, 1 yd (skirt layer)
   black textured, 1 yd (skirt layer)
   candy-corn print ½ yd (knickers)
   light green, 1 yd (body pieces)
   red 4" x 6"
   white 4" x 8"
Felts: black, brown
Fray preventive
Glue
Iron & ironing board
Knitting needle
Needle
Pins
Ribbons: black, green, orange, purple
Scissors
Sewing machine
Striped socks
Threads: black crochet, quilting
White pom-poms, 3mm

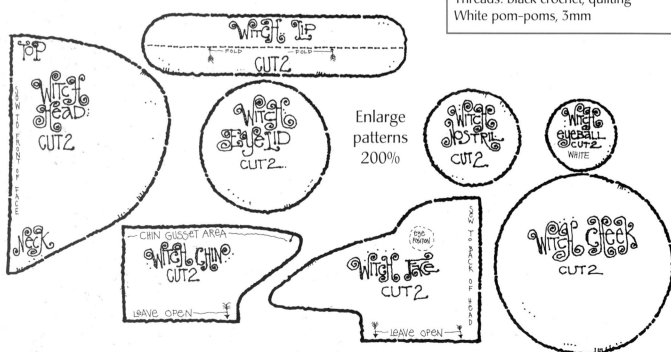

Glue red fabric to card stock and let dry between two heavy objects to flatten. Enlarge and cut out all Witch patterns on pages 84 and 90. Cut out witch's chin, face, gusset, and head from light green fabric. Using sewing machine, sew pieces together, with ¼" seams. Sew gusset into bottom of chin. Sew face, then chin to back of head. Clip and turn. Stuff tip of nose with cotton ball. Stuff rest of head tightly with batting. Leave opening in stuffing for mouth inside.

Cut out mouth inside from red fabric-covered card stock. Fold in half, fabric sides together, and place in face. Stuff head more if necessary. Remove mouth and clip short slits for tabs along edges. Fold tabs under and apply fray preventive if necessary. Place mouth in face and add stuffing around lip area. Pin face to tabs and stitch around mouth edge with tiny invisible stitches.

Fold lips in half lengthwise. Sew and stuff. Hide sewn seam while hand-stitching lips to face. Glue tiny white pom-poms to inside of mouth for teeth—do not make them perfect.

Using patterns on page 84, cut out eyelids, eyeballs (white), nostrils, and cheeks. Refer to How to Stitch on page 93. Gather-stitch around edges. Stuff, close, and knot. Pin and stitch in place. Apply small amount of glue to base of black head on pin and insert for eye pupil. Note: Two different sizes make her look more demented. Stitch black crochet thread around eyes, leaving ¾" tails for eyelashes.

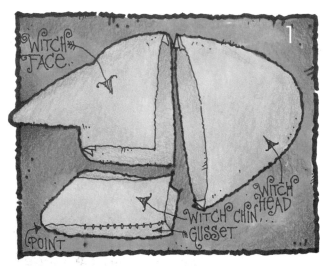

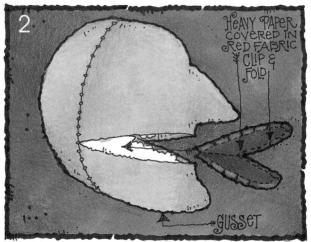

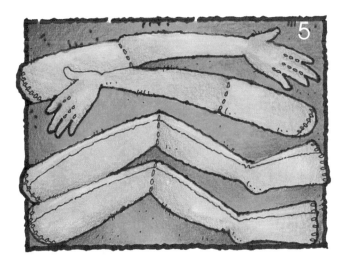

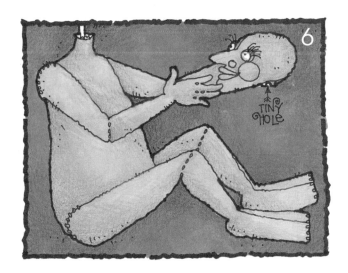

Cut out body pieces from light green fabric. Using sewing machine and ¼" seams, sew, clip, and turn all parts. Stuff tightly except at elbows and knees. Stitch finger detail with quilting thread. Stitch through elbows and knees so they bend. Stitch arms and legs into indicated holes.

Push dowel through neck. Stuff tightly around dowel. Cut a small hole in head. Separate batting with knitting needle so dowel will go through. Securely stitch head to body.

Wrap yarn around book lengthwise approximately 100 times. Hand-stitch through all strands at top of book, back and forth until a solid hair part is formed. Clip loops along bottom of book.

Glue or hand-stitch hair part to top center of head. Trim hair evenly just above shoulders.

Cut two 17" x 19" pieces of candy-corn fabric for knickers. Fold in half lengthwise and, beginning at bottom of fold, cut out 2"-wide x 8"-long strip, rounding at top of strip. With right sides together, stitch sides and inside legs. Clip, turn, and press. Press top down 1". Tuck and sew raw edge under ¼" to make casing. Thread elastic through casing and sew ends together. Place knickers on witch, fray leg bottoms ¼"–½", and tie with three colors of ribbon approximately 1" up.

Cut two 7" x 20" pieces for sleeves. Fold each piece in half lengthwise. Sew seam along each long edge. Fold and stitch one end up ½" for elastic casing. Gather-stitch the other end for shoulder. Turn and press.

Cut black fabric 16" x 19" for bodice. Fold in half to 8" x 19". Cut a small hole in the center of fold, and cut from hole to bottom of one layer. Place bodice piece over shoulders and fold over in front. Fray outside edges. Bottom will tuck into knickers.

Thread elastic through casing at wrist and sew ends together. Make a variety of shapes (triangles, squares folded in fourths, squares with three sides frayed, etc.) and stitch, on top of sleeve at shoulder. Sew sleeves in place. Secure front of bodice, using beads, buttons, or pom-poms.

Make skirt layers, using dimensions in illustration 12, below. Leave all seams in front with a 3" opening. Gather together to fit waist. Cut 4" x 32" waistband. Fray on ends and one long side. Place and sew waistband to skirt, with wrong sides together. Fold band to front and hand-stitch while adding beads.

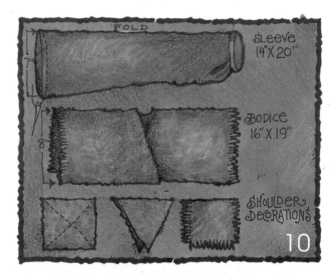

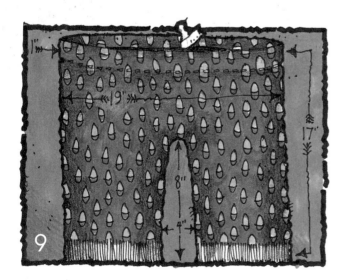

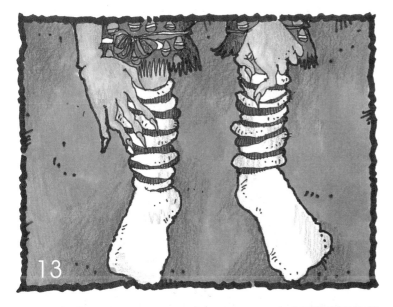

13

Stitch striped socks to backs of ankles and knees, baggy is good. 13

Cut two black and two brown witch shoe toe patterns on page 90. Cut two brown soles and glue to black craft foam. Glue all felt pieces together, black to brown. Sew one shoe toe to each sole, gathering around toe. Blanket-stitch around outside toe edges. 14

Fold back of shoe down, pin in place, and stitch together at sides. Blanket-stitch around outside heel edges. Tie with black and orange ribbons. 15

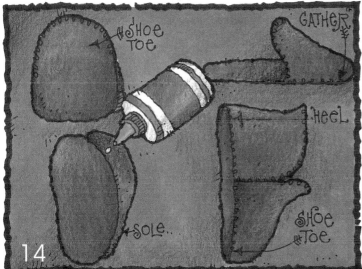

SHOE TOE

GATHER

HEEL

SOLE

SHOE TOE

14

FOLD OVER

15

89

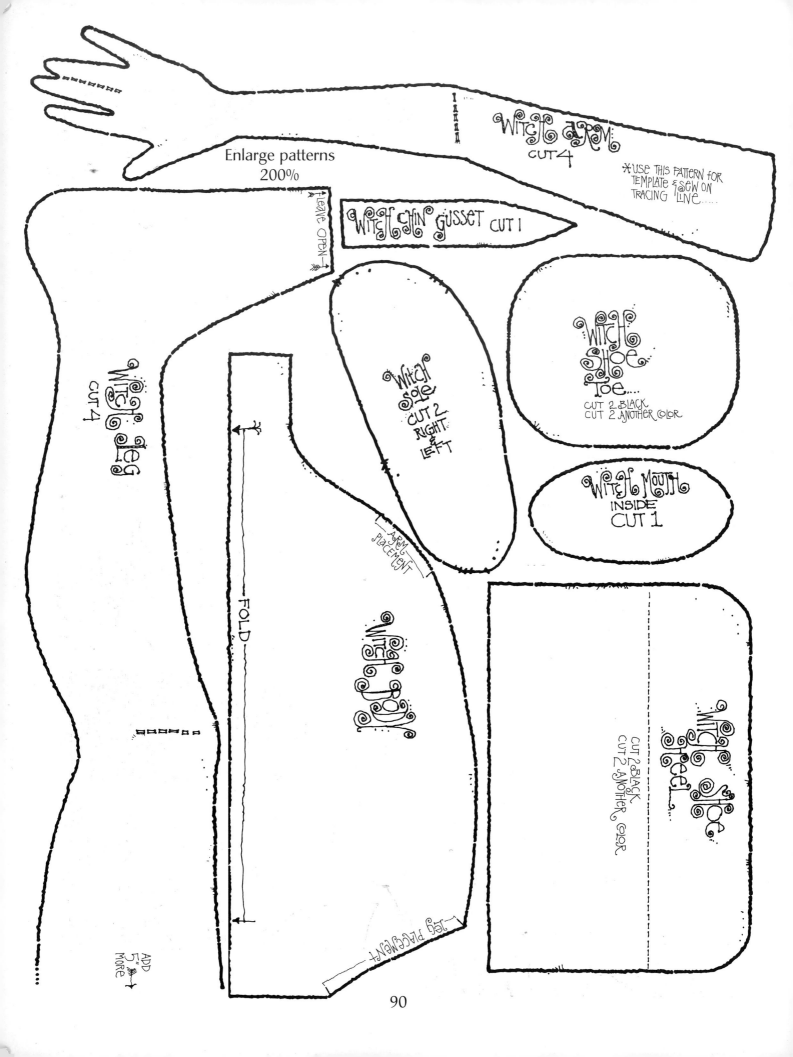

Enlarge patterns
200%

WITCH ARM
CUT 4

*USE THIS PATTERN FOR
TEMPLATE & SEW ON
TRACING LINE......

LEAVE OPEN →

WITCH CHIN GUSSET CUT 1

WITCH
SHOE
TOE....

CUT 2 BLACK
CUT 2 ANOTHER COLOR

WITCH LEG
CUT 4

WITCH
SOLE
CUT 2
RIGHT
&
LEFT

WITCH MOUTH
INSIDE
CUT 1

FOLD

ARM PLACEMENT

WITCH FACE

WITCH HEEL
CUT 2 BLACK
CUT 2 ANOTHER COLOR

LEG PLACEMENT

ADD
5"
MORE

90

Cut tiny circle from center of one foam circle to form brim. Adhere black tulle onto both sides of brim. Stitch and bead around outside edge.

Cut a line up to center of second foam circle. Form foam circle into a cone, then fit cone to witch's head and pin. Cover with black tulle, then stitch and bead along seam. Center cone on hat brim and lightly trace around it. Cut out center. Sew cone to brim while adding beads.

Cut 24" pieces of ribbon, in a variety of colors. Stitch equal amounts of ribbon to each side of inside brim. Place hat on head and tie under chin.

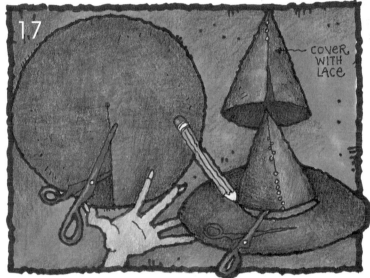

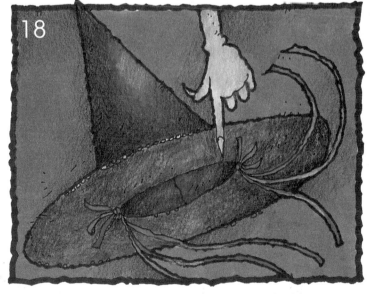

GENERAL INSTRUCTIONS

HOW TO PAINT

* GREAT FLAT WHITE BASE
* CLEANS UP WITH WATER
* COLORS GO ON FLAT
* WORKS ON WOOD · FABRIC · STONE · CLAY

GESSO

ACRYLIC — CLEANS UP WITH WATER
TUBE
JAR
COLORS BLEND WELL

SPONGES — DAB ON PAINT.
BRUSHES — PAINT BASE COLOR OR DETAIL.
STENCILS — READY MADE OR CUT THEM OUT OF PLASTIC.

* DON'T LEAVE BRUSHES IN THE PAINT.
* WHEN MIXING COLORS — MIX MORE THAN ENOUGH — IT WON'T MATCH IF YOU NEED TO MIX MORE.
* ACRYLICS DRY QUICKLY
* CLEAN UP EXTRA PAINT WITH PAPER TOWEL — PAINT WILL CLOG THE SINK.

HOW TO PAPIER MACHE

WALL PAPER PASTE
WHEAT PASTE
FLOUR
WATER
FABRIC STARCH
PAINT

Inflate balloon. Mix fabric starch, flour, wallpaper paste, or wheat paste with water until desired consistency. Tear newspaper into strips. Dip strips, one at a time, into mixture then run between fingers to eliminate excess. Cover entire balloon with strips. Leave small opening around knot. Hang and let dry. Repeat with more newspaper. Let dry. Pop and remove balloon. Cover again with torn strips of white paper. Let dry.

HOW TO STITCH...

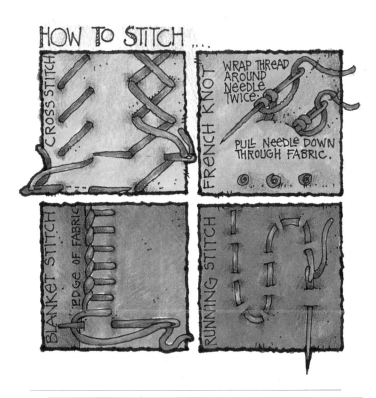

CROSS STITCH

FRENCH KNOT
WRAP THREAD AROUND NEEDLE TWICE.
PULL NEEDLE DOWN THROUGH FABRIC.

BLANKET STITCH
EDGE OF FABRIC

RUNNING STITCH

HOW TO MAKE FOREBODING DOUGH

2 C FLOUR
1 C SALT
2 T COOKING OIL
1¼ C WATER
MIX
KNEAD
KNITTING NEEDLE
PAPER CLIP
SPRAY VARNISH

Mix ingredients. Knead into dough. Use cookie cutters or sculpt into desired shapes. Either insert paper clip into top to hang, or poke hole through shape with knitting needle to string. Let dry. Paint with acrylics and spray varnish.

dem-dough-bones

Materials
Acrylic paints: black, white
Assorted beads with large holes
Butter knife
Foreboding Dough
Metal knitting needles (2)
Oven
Paint brush
Pencil
Ribbons or yarns (2–3 yds each color)

Pinch off golf-ball-sized piece of dough, keeping fingers moist and remaining dough in airtight container. When smoothing dough or attaching pieces together, use a drop of water. Shape dough into skull shapes. Push skull shapes onto knitting needle. Using butter knife, make face and teeth features. Using pencil tip, make eye sockets. Continue making skulls until the desired odd number of skulls are on knitting needle. Repeat process to make even number of bones on another knitting needle. Bake skulls and bones at 250°F until hard.

When hard and cool remove from knitting needles. Paint skulls and bones white or leave natural. Paint eye sockets and teeth black.

Alternately thread bones and skulls onto several lengths of colored ribbons or yarns with knots and assorted beads to decorate.

LETTERS & NUMBERS

ABCDEFGHIJK
LMNOPQRSTU
VWXYZ123456
7890

Lettering should not be a terrifying task. Enlarge or reduce, depending on the needs of your project.

METRIC CONVERSIONS

inches	mm	cm	inches	cm	inches	cm
⅛	3	0.3	9	22.9	30	76.2
¼	6	0.6	10	25.4	31	78.7
⅜	13	1.3	12	30.5	33	83.8
½	16	1.6	13	33.0	34	86.4
⅝	19	1.9	14	35.6	35	88.9
¾	22	2.2	15	38.1	36	91.4
⅞	25	2.5	16	40.6	37	94.0
1	32	3.2	17	43.2	38	96.5
1¼	38	3.8	18	45.7	39	99.1
1½	44	4.4	19	48.3	40	101.6
2	51	5.1	20	50.8	41	104.1
2½	64	6.4	21	53.3	42	106.7
3	76	7.6	22	55.9	43	109.2
3½	89	8.9	23	58.4	44	111.8
4	102	10.2	24	61.0	45	114.3
4½	114	11.4	25	63.5	46	116.8
5	127	12.7	26	66.0	47	119.4
6	152	15.2	27	68.6	48	121.9
7	178	17.8	28	71.1	49	124.5
8	203	20.3	29	73.7	50	127.0

¼ cup — 60 ml
½ cup — 120 ml
1 cup — 240 ml

INDEX